First I win a contest that
makes me a TV star.
Then I get to do some of
the most awesome extreme
sports in the world. And my
two best friends get
to come along for the ride.
How lucky am I?

First published in Great Britain in 2005 by
RISING STARS UK LTD.
76 Farnaby Road, Bromley, BR1 4BH

First published in Australia by Scholastic Australia in 2004.
Text copyright © Philip Kettle, 2004.

A Black Hills book, produced by black dog books

Designed by Blue Boat Design
Cover photo: Blue Boat Design

For more information visit our website at:
www.risingstars-uk.com

British Library Cataloguing in Publication Data

A CIP record for this book is available from the British Library

ISBN 1 905056 47 8

Printed by Bookmarque Ltd, Croydon, Surrey

THE XTREME WORLD OF BILLY KOOL

by Phil Kettle

book:08
rock climbing

RISING ★ STARS

CONTENTS

ROCK CLIMBING EQUIPMENT

Harness

The harness is fastened around your waist and legs and is connected to a rope to keep you from falling.

Helmet

A helmet will protect your head if you happen to fall or bump your head on the rock face.

Ropes

Very durable ropes are used for climbing. They usually have a stretch factor of between ten and fifteen per cent.

Chalk Bag
This is attached to the climber's harness so they can apply chalk to their hands for grip.

Belay Device
The belay device is used by the belayer to control the rope when their partner is climbing.

Camming Device
A camming device can be used as an anchor on a top-rope set up.

Lockgate Karabiner
The gate of these karabiners lock, ensuring that the rope will not slip out.

Climbing Shoes
Special rubber-soled shoes are used when rock climbing to give you the grip you need.

THE END

I was really down. When I felt down,
I always ended up going to the
same place. When I climbed into the
tree house, I was a bit surprised to
find that Nathan was already there.

'What are you doing here?' I asked.

'I just thought it would be a good
place to be,' he said.

'Me too,' I said. I sat down on the
floor of the tree house.

'Do you want to see if you can drop
spit into the ant holes?' I asked.

It had been ages since we'd been to the tree house, just before we went whitewater rafting. We would be shooting the last episode of *The Xtreme World of Billy Kool* on Saturday.

It was good to know that I could still come to the tree house. Even though lots had happened since those first episodes, nothing had really changed.

'I reckon I can drop a spit in an ant hole before you,' said Nathan.

'I wouldn't be too sure of that.'

Nathan was just about to drop his first liquid bomb, when we heard a voice from the bottom of the ladder.

'Some things never change. Just

when I thought that both of you might have grown up, I see that you're still doing the same immature things you always did.'

It was Sally. Like us, she'd felt like coming to the tree house. She said she thought we might have been here.

'So, do you want to have a go?' Nathan asked.

'I will, but only to prove that I'm better than both of you.'

She lay on the floor and stuck her head over the side.

We dropped spit bombs into the ant holes till our mouths became so dry that we couldn't make any more spit to drop.

HOW COOL IS THIS?

I guess we were all a bit down
because the show was going to finish
next week. I wondered whether
we would just go back to being the
same as we were before the show
had started.

Nathan said that he was going to
spend a lot of time with his dad and
that they were going to go on a
camping and whitewater rafting
adventure.

'Dad has rung me every day since
he came to visit. He's trying to move

back here so that he can be closer to me,' Nathan said.

When the show finished I was planning to spend a lot of time with my grandad. He had asked me to help him paint his house and he wanted to get his garden going again. He was going to drive over to pick me up.

The owner of the monster told us that the monster had a brother who needed a good home. When I told dad, he agreed that it would be a good idea for Grandad to have the dog. I don't think Dad really knew how big the monster was till he saw him.

'Grandad is going to have a lot of

fun with the monster's brother, if he's as big as the monster,' Dad said when he first saw him. We planned to give Grandad his new dog when he came to pick me up. I had already thought of a name for the dog. I was going to tell Pop that he should call him 'Mate' because I hoped the dog would be his best mate.

Sally said that she was just going to hang out. 'I'm going to help my dad at his work and I really want to get some study done for school next year,' she said.

Nathan and I just looked at each other when she said that. We both knew that was exactly what Sally would do.

'I don't know why we're all looking so sad,' said Sally. 'We still have one more show to go.'

'Yeah, I've always wanted to go rock climbing,' I said.

'We should all be pretty good at it, I reckon,' Nathan said.

'Yeah—all the time we've spent climbing trees,' I said.

'I hope that when you're climbing the rock face, you both remember where you are.'

'Why would we forget?' I asked Sally.

'You and Nathan might think that you're still in the tree house. If you look down and think the people below are ants, you might spit on them!' she said.

'Yeah, right, as if we'd do that. But wait a minute, if we did, it could be a lot of fun,' I said.

Nathan laughed. He said that there would be no chance of us doing another series if we did that, especially if the spit landed on the director.

JUST ANOTHER SHOW

Before the first few shows I had been really nervous. I never told Nathan or Sally, but sometimes I think that I was even scared. But with the last couple of shows, I hadn't been scared and was really starting to enjoy what we did.

Before we started the TV show, the older kids at school used to call me a little nerd. I think that I used to believe what they said.

Now, I never thought of myself as a nerd. I really believed I was as good as most people at most things.

Last week when Basher Brown had bowled to me at Basher Park, I hit the ball out of the park and into the monster's backyard.

It didn't seem quite the same now that we personally knew the monster. The fear factor had gone. The monster came running out of his yard with the ball in his mouth.

We found out that the monster had a real name, Major. After that we put 'Major' in front of 'monster' so we now called him Major Monster.

But I was really pleased to be able to hit Basher out of the park. Basher thought that maybe I should join his proper cricket team that played on Saturdays in the summer.

I reckon that I would probably be okay if I did. I am a lot more confident than I was before I started doing extreme sports.

Even Mrs Crabtree, our French teacher, told me that she was pleased with how well I was doing in her class.

All I needed for life to be perfect was Crystal to tell me that she would really like to go out with me. I wondered what I would do if she did. Where would I take her? That wasn't something that I was going to have to worry about. There was no chance it would ever happen. That was probably good anyway. What would I say to her?

Maybe I could ask her to come to our tree house and see if she could spit into the ant holes.

It all sounded way too hard. Maybe I should just hope that the production team would decide to have another series of *The Xtreme World of Billy Kool*. Doing even the wildest extreme sport would have to be a lot easier than having a girlfriend.

I guess Nathan, Sally and I knew that we were never going to use our tree house as much as we had done. But I still don't think that we were ready to forget about it or pull it down.

CAST AND
CREW MEETING

On Friday afternoon, before the
limo came to pick us up for the
cast and crew meeting, I watched
the videos of all our shows. It was
strange to look back and see myself
fall out of the raft when we went
whitewater rafting. We all looked a
bit scared before we bungy jumped.
And we looked really scared before
we went skydiving. The last shows
were a lot better than the early ones.
We all seemed a lot more confident.

I now know where to look when I am talking to the cameras and when the director speaks I move and react a lot more quickly than I did when we first started the shows.

The limo pulled up at the front door. Nathan and Sally were already in it. Everyone was pretty quiet on the way.

When the limo pulled up at the studio, there was a massive sign on the front of the building. It said, 'Congratulations Billy, Nathan and Sally.' And in smaller letters it said, 'We'll miss you.' It was signed by all the crew.

'Alright, people,' the director said. 'I know this is the last show but we've still got to concentrate.'

One of the camera crew yelled, 'Make another series.'

'It's had fantastic ratings,' the director said. 'So we might just do that. But now we've got to sort out everything for tomorrow. The rock face is two hours away, so the limo will be picking up the three of you at 7 o'clock. Did you know that climbing routes have names?'

We all shook our heads.

'Well,' the director said, 'on the wall where we're shooting, there are six routes. Danger Bird, RIP, Hard Times, It'll End in Tears, The Only Way is Up and Mr Splat. We've left it up to you to choose which one you want to do. What do you think?'

'Isn't there one with a good name?' Sally asked. 'Like "You will definitely get to the top of this climb"? Or "Heroes"?'

The director shook his head. In the end we chose 'The Only Way is Up.' But not because we thought it sounded good. It was just that every other choice sounded much worse.

THE CLIMB

On Saturday morning, Mum and Dad wished me good luck as I walked out the front door. The limousine from the studio was parked in front of our house. Nathan and Sally were already in the car.

'How bad is it going to be at the end of this when we haven't got an extreme sport to go to,' said Nathan.

'We were lucky to do even these,' Sally said.

Sally had the most amazing attitude to everything that we did. She was always positive. I wondered whether all girls were like Sally.

'We've got to make today's show the best show we've ever done,' Sally said.

The two hours passed pretty quickly. The limo pulled up at a carpark, and Shey was there to take us to the rock face. It was a ten-minute walk through bush. Then, in front of us was a massive rock face. From where we were standing it looked like Mount Everest.

'Don't worry,' Shey said. 'You'll only be climbing as high as twenty metres.'

We got dressed in shorts, harnesses and special climbing shoes with rubber soles. They were the smallest shoes I'd ever seen. Shey said that they'd help us to grip the wall.

When we walked up to the rock face, the crew let out a massive cheer.

'Are you three ready for the last show?' the director asked.

'Ready as we'll ever be,' I answered.

'Alright then, let's make it the best one.'

Location Map

1. Top-rope anchor, attached at four separate points—a tree, a chain bolted to the rock, and to two camming devices in rock cracks

2. The crux—the hardest part of the climb

3. The climbing route, 'The Only Way is Up'

4. The climbing route, 'Danger Bird'

5. The belayer

6. Sound crew based for monitoring

④

Our Equipment

Camming Device

Rope

Chalk Bag

Harness

Climbing Shoes

Lockgate Karabiner

Belay Device

Helmet

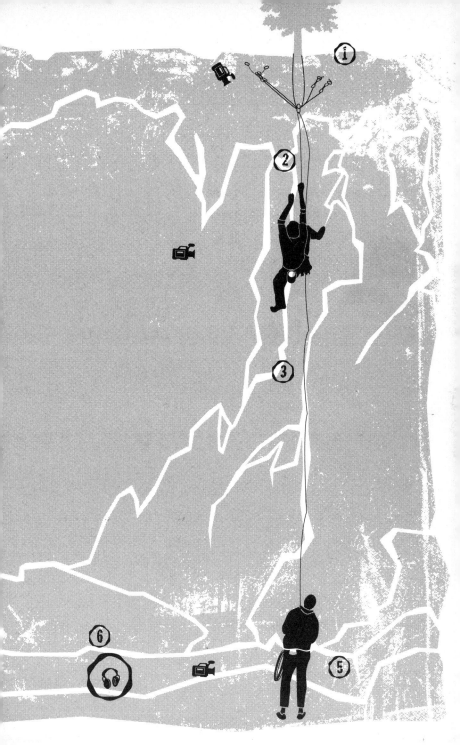

LIGHTS, CAMERA, ACTION

BILLY
My name is Billy Kool.
With my best friends Sally
and Nathan, we are the
hosts of this fantastic
show, *The Xtreme World of
Billy Kool*. Today we are
rock climbing.

NATHAN
I'm really looking forward
to climbing. I reckon
we'll get to feel what
it's like to be a spider.

SALLY
Nathan, I hope my mum
doesn't see you. You
should see what she does
to spiders on the wall.

NATHAN
And what's that?

SALLY
Squish,squash.

BILLY
With us, for the last show in *The Xtreme World of Billy Kool,* is Shey, our safety co-ordinator and extreme sport expert.

SHEY
Hi, Billy, and welcome to all our viewers. Rock climbing, whether indoors or outdoors, is one of the most physically demanding extreme sports there is.

NATHAN
So then I will be really good at climbing.

SALLY
Maybe you will, Nathan.

I've seen you climb a tree
and you're pretty good at
that.

SHEY
Rock climbing is a lot
different to climbing a
tree. To become really
skilled you need to train
a lot. Rock climbing is a
physical and mental
challenge. It's a lot
harder than it looks.

BILLY
We have already practised
through the week on an
indoor wall. So we're
ready to climb. An anchor
system has been set up at
the top of the climb. The
rope is anchored in four
different places-a tree,
a chain, and two cracks in

the rock face. That means we'll be very safe. We'll attach the rope to the harnesses we're wearing. The rope will be attached with a figure-eight knot, one of the safest knots around.

SHEY
The ropes safeguard us in case we fall.

NATHAN
Will it hurt if we fall?

SHEY
When we climb, we do it in teams. One person climbs and the other person stays on the ground. That person is called the belayer.

BILLY
That's a funny name.

SHEY
The rope is connected to the anchor system Billy was just talking about. Then one end of the rope is attached to the harness the climber is wearing. The other end of the rope is attached to the harness the belayer is wearing. As the climber moves up the wall, the rope gets slack. It's the belayer's job to pull the rope tight, so if the climber falls, they'll be caught by the rope.

SALLY
So the belayer makes sure that the person who is climbing won't get hurt if they fall.

NATHAN
They won't have to worry
about me. I'll climb up
the wall like a spider.

BILLY
We'll soon find out
because you're going
first.

SHEY
Make sure that you put
plenty of chalk on your
hands before you start.

SALLY
Chalk absorbs sweat and
prevents your fingers from
slipping.

*SHEY belays for NATHAN.
She threads one end of the
rope though her harness
and the belay device that*

she'll use to control the rope. She also clips her harness into an anchor system that is attached to the ground. That means that if Nathan falls, Shey will be able to control it and won't get pulled into the air herself. The other end of the rope is threaded through Nathan's harness and secured with a figure-eight knot.

SHEY
Okay, Nathan, you are on belay. Climb when ready.

BILLY
That means that Nathan can start climbing. Each time someone begins a climb, the belayer will say that so the climber knows

they are safe to climb.
The climber will answer,
'climbing'.

NATHAN
Climbing.

BILLY
We are watching as Nathan
prepares to climb to the
top of the rock face. It's
about twenty metres high.
From down here, it doesn't
look that far.

SALLY
But it will feel like
forever. There are no
branches to rest on if you
get tired.

NATHAN
This will require all my
strength and balance.

Nathan reaches above his head. There is a part of the rock sticking out that he can hold. He steps onto a foothold that is knee-high off the ground.

NATHAN
I've only just got off the ground and already my hands are starting to ache. It's hard to find good holds.

SHEY
Concentrate and keep going. I've got you. A hold is what Nathan is using to get up the rock face. Holds are literally what Nathan 'holds' onto.

Nathan manages to get

another few metres up before he slips and falls. Shey has been keeping the rope tight so he only falls a couple of centimetres. She lowers him down.

NATHAN
How hard was that! I thought I would be able to climb the wall like a spider. But that's a lot harder than anything that I have ever done. My arms are killing me.

SHEY
Now that we have seen how hard it is to climb, let's see how far Sally can get.

SALLY
I just hope that I get
higher than Nathan did.

*The rope is secured to
SALLY'S harness and she
and Shey go through safety
checks.*

SHEY
On belay. Climb when
ready.

SALLY
Climbing.

BILLY
Go Sally.

*Sally moves slowly up the
rock. After a few metres
her legs begin to shake.*

SALLY
It wasn't so bad at first,
but the rock is really
hard and my hands are
starting to hurt. My legs
are getting a bit shaky
too, but I want to get
up higher than Nathan did.

SHEY
You've got past where
Nathan fell. Good work,
Sally.

BILLY
You're getting really high
now.

SALLY
Lucky I'm not scared of
heights! Oh, I'm stuck!
I can't see where to put
my hands next.

NATHAN
There's a hold just above your head, a little to the right.

SALLY
That's not a hold. That's a piece of chewing gum! My arms are really aching. I don't know if I can hold on—aaahhhhhhhhhh!

Sally falls off and is lowered back to the ground.

SHEY
Good climb, Sally.

BILLY
As you can see, it's harder than it looks. It's my turn. I'm determined to get to the top.

Shey belays for Billy.

SHEY
So, are you ready to start?

BILLY chalks his hands and grits his teeth. He moves to the rock face.

SHEY
On belay. Climb when ready.

BILLY
Climbing.

SALLY
Billy looks really determined.

NATHAN
Yes, he does. He's not even talking.

BILLY
That's right!

SHEY
Billy has made it past
where Nathan fell off.
Keep going, Billy.

NATHAN
You're almost at the same
place Sally fell off.
Don't look down.

BILLY
Shhhhhh.

*Everyone falls silent.
The camera crew are
totally focused on Billy.
The director stands very
still. Everyone seems
to have realised that
something special is
happening with Billy.*

NATHAN
Billy has got past the
chewing gum hold. He's
getting closer. About five
metres away from the top.
From down here, he kind of
looks like a spider.

BILLY
This is really hard.
My arms, my legs and
my fingers are really
hurting. But I really want
to make it to the top.

SALLY
You can do it, Billy.

NATHAN
Yeah, make sure that you
get to the top.

SHEY
Don't look down. Keep concentrating.

BILLY
Ahhhhhhh!

Billy's hand slips. He is dangling from the wall by one hand, but he is able to get another grip. He only has about a metre to go.

NATHAN
He must be really starting to hurt now.

SALLY
He's going to make it.

Billy's hand reaches over the top. The camera crew at the top of the climb start clapping.

BILLY
Wow, how great is this!
I've made it to the top.
Every bit of my body
hurts.

*Shey lowers Billy back
down to the ground. He
unties the figure-eight
knot and sits down on the
ground.*

SHEY
Well done, Billy.

BILLY
That was awesome. My arms
and legs are shaking so
much I have to sit down. I
still can't believe that I
made it to the top.

NATHAN
Well, you did and that was

great. I thought you were
going to come off for a
second, but you didn't.

SALLY
Finally, you beat me at
something.

BILLY
I'm pleased that I made
it to the top. But I'm
a bit sad too, because
this brings us to the end
of another show. And it
brings us to the end of
the series. My name is
Billy Kool and this has
been the last episode of
*The Xtreme World of Billy
Kool.* My name is Billy
Kool and, until we meet
again, goodbye.

DIRECTOR
Cut. That's a wrap, well done, Billy, that was fantastic.

All the crew gather around and shake Billy, Nathan and Sally's hands.

SALLY
I want to climb again. If Billy can get to the top, so can I.

NATHAN
And I want to do it again too. Are you coming, Billy?

BILLY
It's all yours. My fingers
are so sore I can barely
move them. I'll watch from
down here.

Doing *The Xtreme World of Billy Kool* was awesome. All the sports I did are my favourites—they're each as good as the other. Extreme sports are fantastic.

It felt really good to get to the top of the climb, especially after getting dumped out of the raft when we went whitewater rafting, and crashing when we went snowboarding and kart racing.

I'm glad that I don't get as nervous as I used to. Being able to do extreme sports has made me more confident. Not confident enough to ask Crystal out, but at least I can say hello to her now.

I hope that the production company decides to make another series. Nathan and Sally and I are going to talk to the producer about other sports we could do, like hang-gliding and canyoning. Awesome.

In the meantime I'm going down to Basher Park. I'm going to see if I can hit Basher for a six.

Dear Billy, Sally & Nathan

Last week I went to a Rodeo
and watched the bull riding.
Bull riding is really extreme.
My dad rode one of the bulls,
and fell off. We all laughed,
but he didn't. He's been in bed
for two weeks with a really
sore leg.

Emily, your biggest fan

Extreme Information
History

Rock climbing grew out of mountain climbing and mountaineering.

People have been climbing mountains throughout history for conquest, for exploration and for religious reasons. But it wasn't until 1786 that mountain climbing became firmly established when Mont Blanc, the highest mountain in Western Europe, was climbed.

In the 1800s, basic rope techniques were developed to aid mountaineers over steep sections of rock. By the late 1800s, rock climbing had become an activity within itself. In England, climbs

were graded to reflect their difficulty.
Back then, climbers wore leather boots
with exposed nails to help them grip the
rock, or sometimes socks on the outsides
of their shoes. Around the turn of the
century, Europeans developed karabiners.

Rock climbing, as we know it today,
began to evolve. In the 1920s, better
footwear was developed and climbing
took off in the United States. During
World War II, nylon ropes were
developed.

In the 1950s and 1960s, rock climbing
standards rose dramatically. In the 1980s
sticky rubber shoes emerged. Sport-
climbing was developed, which made
climbing safer and climbers could work
on harder routes. Indoor climbing gyms

were developed in the 1990s, which
opened up the sport to many more people.

There are many types of climbing:
bouldering, ice climbing, sport climbing,
traditional climbing, indoor climbing.
Rock climbing uses more muscles than
any other sport or activity. It is an
extreme challenge, both physically and
mentally.

Glossary

Anchor

Where the rope is secured to the rock.

Biner

Short for karabiner

Bomb-proof

Very secure, very solid, fail-safe — could be used to refer to a hold or an anchor.

Boulder

A rock or boulder short enough to climb safely without a rope.

Crag

Name for a small climbing area.

Crank

To pull on a hold as hard as you can.

Crimper

A tiny, sharp edge.

Crux

The most difficult part of the climb.

'Falling'

Yelled when a climber is about to fall, to alert the belayer.

Fist jam

Jamming the fist into a crack.

Gumby

A name for a beginner climber.

Hold

Any part of the rock which the climber can grip with their hands or feet.

Jug

A large, secure hold.

Karabiner

A springloaded metal clip designed for joining ropes together, or a rope to a harness.

Lead

To go first up a rock face, without being on top-rope.

Pro/protection

Anchors placed during the climb to protect the leader.

Pumped

Tired forearms.

Screamer

A very long fall.

Sewing-machine leg or arm

A leg or arm under tension that suddenly begins jerking up and down like a sewing machine. It happens when muscles get tired.

Top-rope

Where the rope is anchored at the top of the climb—beginners use this set up.

Equipment

Harness

The most popular harness is a waist belt with separate leg loops. For safety the waist loop buckle is doubled back on itself. The leg loops are padded for comfort. Harnesses have a life-span of three to four years. They must be replaced after this for safety reasons.

Shoes

Climbing shoes are very tight fitting, with rubber soles that help climbers grip the rock.

Helmet

Helmets are an absolute must when climbing. Modern helmets are well-designed, light, ventilated and comfortable to wear. They will protect you if you fall or hit your head on the rock face.

Chalk

'Chalk' is powdered magnesium carbonate. It looks like white powder and is used to keep climber's hands dry.

Rope

Modern climbing ropes are made of a braided nylon core covered by a woven nylon sheath. The core absorbs the force generated by a fall.

PHIL KETTLE

Phil Kettle lives in inner-city Melbourne, Australia. He has three children, Joel, Ryan and Shey. Originally from northern Victoria, Phil grew up on a vineyard. He played football and cricket and loved any sport where he could kick, hit or throw something.

These days, Phil likes to go to the Melbourne Cricket Ground on a winter afternoon and cheer on his favourite Australian Rules team, the Richmond Tigers. Phil hopes that one day he will be able to watch the Tigers win a grand final—'Even if that means I have to live till I'm 100.'

THE Xtreme WORLD OF BILLY KOOL

by Phil Kettle

Billy Kool books are available from most booksellers. For mail order information please call Rising Stars on 01933 443862 or visit www.risingstars-uk.com